MW01611501

My

A love story of a mouse and her car

Written and Illustrated by
Joan C. Gratz

This is a relatively true story. The color of the Tesla has been changed to protect its privacy and for greater graphic impact. The species of the author has been changed for similar reasons.

Copyright Joan C. Gratz
First edition 2014   Published in Portland, Oregon
All rights reserved. No part of this book may be reproduced
without written permission except in the context of reviews.

For information write Gratzfilm 1802 NW Upshur, Portland, OR. 97209

ISBN: 0974832332

Maxine loved shopping at the mall. She was tempted by the discounted unicorns, but was afraid they were past their expiration date.

Maxine was surprised to find a car for sale in the mall.
She was transfixed by its beauty.

Maxine took the Tesla for a test drive. The acceleration was so great she she could scarcely keep her features on her face.

Maxine understood the Tesla to be as magical a creature as the unicorn but one with a more subtle horn and no gas emissions.

Maxine's friends were surprised when she returned with a car.
They hoped she would buy a bargain unicorn.

She and her friends looked everywhere for the engine.
Though the Tesla knew nothing of gas or lubricants,
Maxine suspected the car was still more intelligent than she.

Taking a cue from her new Tesla, Maxine tried to recharge her own batteries.

Both awake and asleep the car permeated
her every thought. Maxine dreamed her
quilt transformed into a Tesla parking lot.

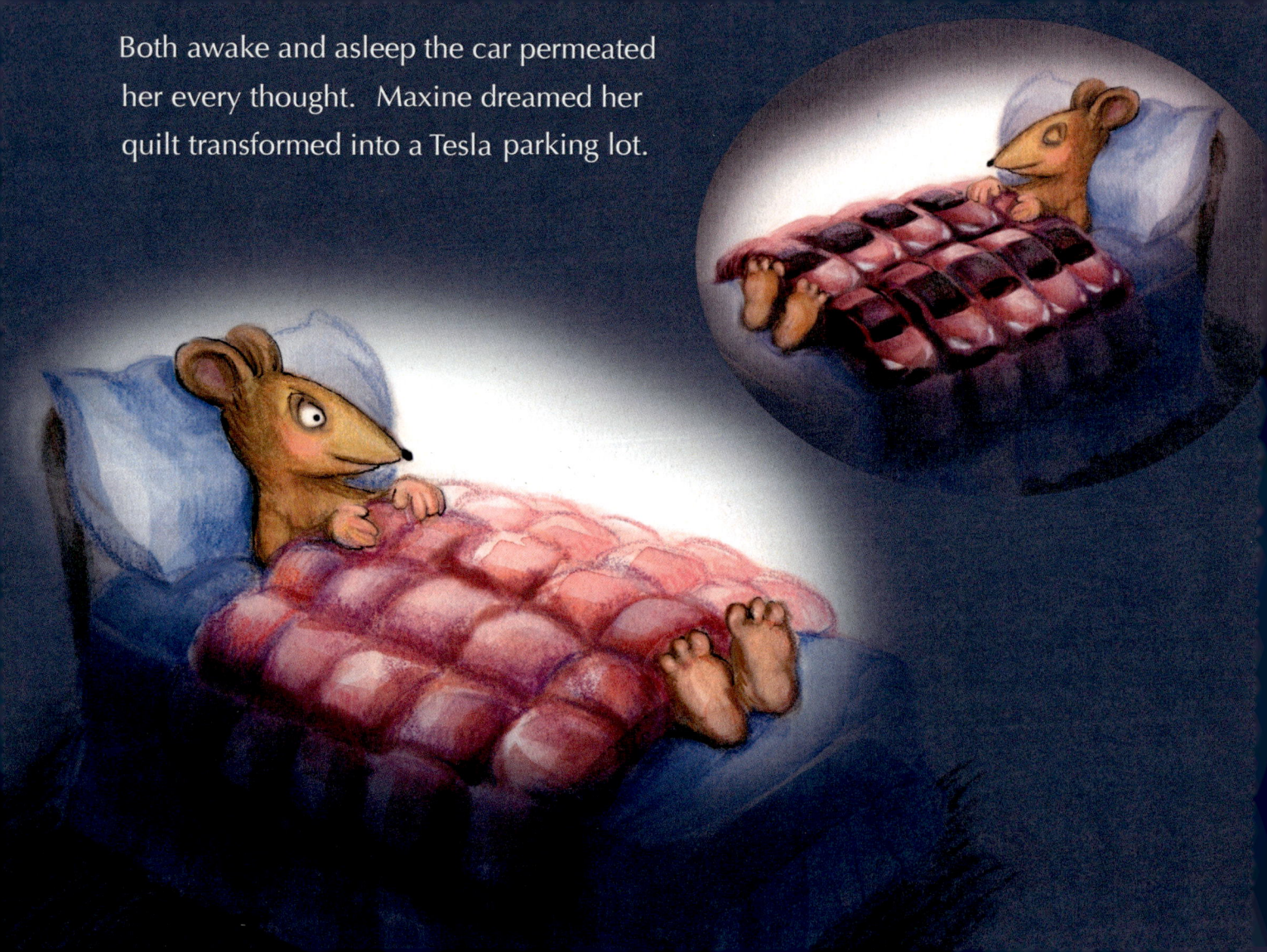

Maxine feared vandals who would spray graffiti, dance a jig,
pretend to be roadkill, or lie about their gas mileage.

Extremely protective, Maxine would not allow babies, people with pastries, or those with mismatched socks to ride in her car. No one had the right qualities for a ride in the Tesla.

Maxine knew her car was so large and precious she should only share the road with Morris Minors, Mini Coopers, mopeds, and unicycles.

Maxine was so protective of her car that driving was impossible.

Eventually Maxine found the perfect parking space,
although she had no desire to be in Death Valley.

Owning a Tesla was not without problems. Maxine sometimes felt she was driving a big bag of cash.

Maxine overdressed to be worthy of her car.

Having a Tesla, Maxine was at the apex of the pyramid.

Maxine imagined she was the life of every party.

Feeling her superiority, Maxine ran for public office. The press had many penetrating though irrelevant questions.

It seemed to Maxine owning a Tesla outshown her many accomplishments.

A benefit of having a Tesla were her many new gentlemen callers.
They were attracted to the Tesla's sleek body, plump electric cord,
and articulated spokes.

Young men in hot muscle cars often challenged her to race.

Maxine's friends thought she was techno-forward and ostentatious, whereas her acquaintances felt she was merely ostentatious.

Maxine knew the path to Nirvana could be found on the Tesla touchscreen.

Having purchased her splendid car, Maxine felt obliged
to those who needed a handout.

The recipient of her charity begged for a ride to the ocean. Maxine refused.
She feared this spineless soul might get ink on her creamy leather seats.

Over time Maxine's worries about vandalism, road sharing, and parallel parking vanished for she knew she owned the world's safest car.

Maxine grew accustomed to her Tesla's comfort, beauty, and energy efficiency.
Was it time to buy a Hummer? Definitely not!

Should Maxine abandon her car, walk everywhere and reconnect with her community? Possibly not.

In the end Maxine realized true happiness comes from sharing what you love, not from living in a cocoon of safety and distant admiration. Maxine invited her friends to ride everywhere with her or at least run along side.

Made in the USA
Monee, IL
08 July 2021

73053264R00021